# DARIO RABOZZI

# MY LIFE IN COLOR

## How To Find Your Way Among Health and Financial Freedom To Live A Fulfilled, Happy Life

Title

"MY LIFE IN COLOR"


Author

Dario Rabozzi


Publisher

Bruno Editore


Website

http://www.brunoeditore.it

*No deep thinker would dare say that the scent of hawthorn is indifferent to the constellations*
Author Francesco Rose, an amazing person I was lucky to share a hospital room with during my illness.

# Table of Contents

# Introduction

This autobiographical book has two goals: it firstly seeks to offer some tools and advice for facing a horrible illness such as cancer, and secondly seeks to offer tools for achieving financial freedom, not necessarily understood as wealth, but as the freedom to better manage your time without being overly constrained by working hours.

I apologize to my readers if my writing style is overly simple: I am not a writer by profession, but a businessman.

2020 was undoubtedly an ominous year, with the waves of Covid-19 seriously changing the world in terms of everything from the economy to health, from education to the social sphere, and everyone's life has been severely affected, regardless of their political beliefs and personal choices.

In addition to the worldwide pandemic, the weather conditions have not been ideal: in the part of Piedmont, Italy where I live, we haven't seen such heavy rain and intense winds for at least fifty years. Thirty-year-old plants have fallen, bridges have collapsed, and houses have been swept away by flooding rivers, creating a nightmare in the provinces of Novara, Verbano-Cusio-Ossola and beyond.

Even considering all the above, I still try to see a positive side in these events in order to avoid becoming depressed and so as to instill inspiration in those fighting all these struggles. I have written a book about myself, about my personality. I believe I have led an extraordinary life and I hope my experience can be useful for people, helping them improve their work, be more satisfied with life, and devote more time to their loved ones.

I would like to thank all those I have met along my way, from family to friends, from roommates to former university-work colleagues who substantially contributed to my education. I do not hold any grudges, even if there may have been some misunderstandings in my past.

I hope to make you smile and give you a little optimism in life with my autobiography, to help you always look on the bright side of things and never give up.

# Chapter 1:
# Relationships and Education

I consider networking and the relationships I have with others to be of great importance, both from a business perspective and for personal growth and education. I consider myself lucky from this point of view. Indeed, I have met people, including family and friends, who have positively contributed to the person I am today. I would like to begin my autobiographical journey by introducing those I hold dearest: my family.

Mamma Caterina is a sprightly lady born in 1948, in defiance to all those who think that people can no longer be productive after the age of seventy. She is originally from Casaletto Spartano but moved to Ameno when still very young, where she worked as a teacher for children attending the activity camps in the municipality of Milan.

She is a very stubborn person and clings very firmly to her beliefs, even if they may be objectively questionable. She was a real force in the education of young people, especially those less fortunate in life.

As a typical woman from the South, she has always had a strong predilection for cooking. It is impossible to be on a diet with her around. She is always worried that you may not be getting enough to eat and is constantly inundating you with prodigious amounts of delicious food. In addition to cooking, she is a very hard worker.

In contrast to Caterina, there is Father Renato. He was very good with his hands and worked for a company that made printing presses for newspapers. He is an animal lover, especially fond of cats, and an avid gardener.

One of his favorite books on how to grow your garden while taking the phases of the moon into account! He is an expert in weather forecasting, mushrooms, Terence Hill movies, and soccer, but Papa Renato is also among the least enthusiastic people in the world.

When you give him a gift or organize something for him, it almost seems as if you're doing him a huge favor judging by the amount of enthusiasm he shows, but we like him that way.

Now we come to my brother Marco. He is seven years younger than me, born in 1990, and someone I could write a whole book about.

One day I said to my mother, who was no longer young, "Mom, the best gift you could give me in the whole, wide world would be a little brother. I would call him Marco, after Marco Van Basten, and Marco, my friend Donato's brother". No sooner said than done! My father and my mother, now 40 years old, managed to conjure up a beautiful child, not without some difficulty, of course.

Marco is very generous but also sometimes very stubborn. That's why we've had quite a few arguments over the years, but they've always been resolved amicably.

In many ways Marco is much more conservative than I am and was accustomed to workplaces which focused on achieving objectives and not meeting deadlines. For example, he worked for a large technology company in America.

Marco and I, together with my friend Michele, founded our present company, as I will describe in the following chapters, and there was a time when, for health reasons, I couldn't work.

Our company has been highly successful because everyone is an expert in their own field; my brother in technology, Michele at product level (he writes and has always had a visceral passion for cars), and me on the commercial and product side. This was the subject I studied, and I gained lot of relevant work experience you could say that I got my hands dirty before founding our company.

I am very annoyed when my brother, friends, or colleagues don't respect our work ethic, when they don't meet deadlines or fail to show respect for others, people who have studied and worked hard in life to create something beautiful, their dream job.

I always say that we have, first and foremost, a job to do. We have always given our employees the best tools to stay up to date with market developments. I have had some disproportionate and adverse reactions from some of them. Sometimes they are insensitive about others' feelings, but I've never felt any resentment towards them, and I have always acted in their best interest, trying to give people work and with it financial security.

Now I'd like to talk about a person who, unfortunately, is no longer with us but who was a real role model for me and for everyone living in Ameno: my Nonno Rocco. He was also from the South, moved to Ameno for work, and lived in a house near the town hall for many years.

He had a great passion for the accordion and carried one around over his shoulder. He would play magical music on the steps of the church in the town center. People would gather around him to listen, attracted to the music like flies to honey. Nonno Rocco would often come with my father and me to fetch water from a local spring. He loved pears and cooked fruit. He also drove a scooter with which he caused a good deal of trouble.

He had prostate problems, and he would often ask my father to take him to the hospital to have his catheter inserted. Then it would bother him and he'd take it out himself. He was a bit nuts.

Nonno Rocco passed away several years ago, but he was always idolized in the town. This was confirmed during a conversation I recently had with the owner of a wine shop, who was very insistent on finding and showing me a photo he had of my grandfather.

My uncle Giovanni is also held in great affection. Giovanni is my mother's brother and lives in Novara. I fondly recall living with him in Novara when I began studying at the university in Milan. I remember taking an old bicycle that had belonged to my father to bike to the station to catch a train to Milan. He is a lot of fun to be with, the type of person who could always put you in a good mood and make you smile. Now I would like to speak about my education and the schools I attended and the friends I made.

I studied at the local school in town. I have fond memories of a school cook who prepared great food and the plays we used to put on with the teachers during the parties we had. I always really liked drama and the theater. One year I played Happy, one of the seven dwarfs. I made friends with several kids who were at elementary school with me. My best friend and closest companion was Donato, Dody to his friends, who was the fourth of five siblings, one girl and four boys. Dody and I were very close, although we drifted apart as time passed. He now works in a restaurant, while I went down a completely different path. But I'm always very happy to see him when all of the old friends meet up for dinner.

Dody and I went to the seaside together several times, more precisely to Rimini and Jesolo, and we had a great time.

After elementary school I went to middle school in Orta. My best friend there was Davide; we sat next to each other in class year after year and also spent a lot of time together out of school. Now he works in the transport sector and promotes of Orta San Giulio, a town in a fantastic part of the country that has, in my opinion, few equals in the world in terms of food and culture.

It was during high school that I honed my skills but also made some mistakes, sometimes going a bit over the top. I went to the Scientific High School in Borgomanero. There were about twenty or so students in the class and my best friend and classmate was Vito, who now works in Swiss health care.

Vito was exceptionally good at Latin. He always let me copy during tests and we always ran to school on the first day to grab the desks at the back. During physics and biology classes, we used to build a barricade around us with books so that we couldn't be seen and we'd play cards. He often came to sleep over at my house. We'd play basketball in my room and shared a passion for soccer (he's a fan of Inter Milan, while I root for Juventus).

In high school we had a very odd Biology professor. Lessons with him were a hoot. Once a group of us were at a friend's house studying math for a text the next day. When we couldn't work out the answers sometimes we'd plan alternative "solutions" to get out of having to take the test. One night I took the chain from my grandfather's scooter and gave it to some friends who locked the school gates with it. The next morning there was a crowd of people at the gate, our test had obviously been postponed (not that I suggest doing this!), and the janitor was struggling to cut through the chain with shears.

I have fond memories of class pizza nights, drinking aperitifs, chatting with great people about their lives and passions. Not to mention the school trips; we'd play around and joke all the time.

I did well in high school and finished with 98/100. I always enjoyed studying. Even if sometimes I stirred up a bit of mischief, I wanted to be at the top of the class in as many subjects as possible. During the last year I took an admissions test at Bocconi. This was a general knowledge exam for a place in the new degree course in Economics for Art, Culture and Communication. I was selected as one of the three hundred to enroll in the course out of thousands of applicants from all over Italy (half of them based on their final grade in high school and the other half based on the Bocconi admissions test).

During this period at Bocconi, I managed to get my head together a little. I was well aware that my parents were making a large financial sacrifice to keep me there, to give me the chance to study and live in Milan. It was really important that I didn't go off the rails. Perhaps in my first year I was still a bit irresponsible. We had a good soccer team and often played in Ravizza Park with unemployed local people, mostly Albanians and North Africans. I had lots of laughs with my university friends Nicola, Alessandro, Gianmario, Marco, Aldo, Fabio, Silvia, Camilla, Giorgio, Salvo, and many others.

I also lived in three different houses, always with other girls: Francesca, Paola, Sabina, Nadia, Elena, Gloria, and Maria.

During this two-year period, I enrolled in the Marketing Management specialization. In the first week I suffered an existential crisis, worried I had gone down the wrong path, both in my studies and in life. I had never made such a clear-cut decision before. My dear friend Nicola greatly helped me through it, and I'll always be grateful to him.

During those two years I had the chance to study at UCLA in Los Angeles for a month. I eagerly seized the opportunity and was able to thanks to my good grades and was awarded a scholarship. It was a fantastic multicultural experience for me. It was 2006, the year that Italy won the World Cup, and a group of us would go down to the bar to watch our national team play. It was a very exciting experience.

After finishing at UCLA, Nicola and I took a car down the Pacific coast of the United States to conquer Mexico! We slept in motels we found on the way. One night we couldn't find a motel and had to sleep in the car in a multi-level parking lot. The most exciting part of the journey was when we crossed the border into Mexico. To get into the country we had to go pass customs, which was surrounded by fences. I especially loved Tijuana, one of the most infamous cities in the world.

I also remember my time in the States for the wonderful trips I took to Bryce Canyon, a small national park in the southwest of the United States, in Utah, with its vivid rock formations ranging in color from red, to orange, to white.

So before going on to discuss my work experience, I'd like to take a brief detour to describe my hobbies and passion.

# Chapter 2:

# Hobbies and Travel

One thing I've always loved is sports in general, both playing them and watching. I played soccer until high school, for the Bolzano Novarese and San Maurizio D'Opaglio teams. I often played as a forward, wearing jersey number 9, and I loved scoring goals. I was always quite a good player, even though our team wasn't ranked very high in the league.

I really enjoyed spending time with my teammates, especially on the bus trips we used to take to Rimini to celebrate New Year's eve.

When I played for San Maurizio, there were a few hot-headed players. Once after a game against Borgo Ticino, the Carabinieri had to be called to escort the visiting team to safety.

In addition to soccer, I've always enjoyed 5-a-side soccer. I had season tickets for Novara Calcio for two years. Rigoni's goal in the 44th minute of the second half in the play-offs against Reggina in order to be promoted to Serie A in 2011 was one of the most exciting moments of my life.

I went to watch Juventus play at the stadium a few times at the beginning of my university studies, and later I got a job at San Siro Stadium and could watch the second half of AC Milan's matches.

I've always also enjoyed playing fantasy soccer with friends, and now it's almost become a job. In 2020-2021 my team is in partnership with my dear friend Stefano, but I'm not entirely convinced by our team. We are used to being in first place.

Still on the topic of sports, I also enjoy tennis, squash, table tennis, sailing, fitness boxing, and swimming.

Music has always been another passion of mine. I'm a big fan of Battiato and have seen him in concert. I'm also a fan of the band Baustelle and the singer-songwriter Ligabue. I also enjoy listening to other genres of music, such as dance music, rock, pop, and the great Italian classics.

Recently, while we were having dinner, my mother thought it was a good idea to play a song on her smartphone as loud as possible, the beautiful "Un giorno mi dirai" by Stadio, winner of the Sanremo Festival 2016. The song talks about the relationship between father and daughter. Given the situation, I decided it was best to let it pass.

I love action movies, comedies (I'm crazy about Zalone), great classics like " There Will Be Blood ", "Donnie Darko", " As Good As It Gets ", and Di Caprio and Cohen brothers' movies.

I really like art and often go to museums. My dream city is Barcelona for its great variety of culture, entertainment, dynamism and, last but not least, its proximity to the sea.

I have always been a fan of cooking, eating well, and trying food from different cultures. One of my favorite things to do is visit a nice holiday farm to enjoy a platter of cured meats and cheeses and a glass of good red wine. I also really enjoy an aperitif with friends.

I was also a bit of a shopaholic. My ex had to bring me suitcases full of stuff I had left in the last house I had lived in with her.

I love nature, animals and, in particular, mushroom hunting.

Now I would like to speak about travel. It is probably my greatest passion, as it combines different cultures, languages, and food.

I started traveling abroad as a child. I enjoyed a study vacation in Ireland in Mullingar, Galway and once in Chester, England. I've always stayed with locals or friends to improve my English.

I particularly remember something that happened in Mullingar. A couple of girls in a mall wolf-whistled at us as a token of their appreciation. In Ireland, young girls are generally much more "playful" than Italians.

In Europe, I have been to Paris, Frankfurt, Greece, Amsterdam, Geneva, Colmar, the Pag Islands in Croatia, Barcelona, Salou, Lloret De Mar, San Sebastien,

Valencia, the French Riviera, Mykonos, Edinburgh, and Warsaw.

In Italy I have often visited Rimini, Jesolo, Lido di Fermo, Sesti Levante, Bormio, the southeast coast of Sardinia, Sant'Antioco, Lecce, Gallipoli, and the beautiful and unique Matera. To these locations can be added several weeks of skiing in Trentino and Sestriere.

As for longer trips abroad, as I mentioned, I studied in Los Angeles, visited Cuba with friends, went to the Bahamas, Miami Beach and, with my former partner, to New York, Japan, and Thailand. In short, I haven't missed out on seeing the world.

**Krakow**

In November 2010, my brother, three friends of mine, Jack, Francesco, and Michele (who we called "the Archaeologist" after his college major) and I spent a long weekend in Krakow.

We stayed in a house near the city's central square and took a day trip to the famous salt mines near Wieliczka, in the Krakow metropolitan area.

The Wieliczka Salt Mine reaches a depth of 327 meters and has 287 kilometers of galleries and tunnels. 3.5 kilometers of them are open to the public and have statues of historical and religious figures, all carved by miners directly into the salt. The crystals from the candlesticks were also forged in the salt.

The mine also has display rooms, chapels, and underground lakes, and you can learn about its history. The Wieliczka mine is commonly known as "the underground salt cathedral of Poland" and has about 800,000 visitors a year. In 1978 the Wieliczka Salt Mine was added to the list of UNESCO World Heritage Sites, and in 2013 the site was extended to include the Bochnia Salt Mine (source: Wikipedia).

The cost of living was quite low in Poland, and the Polish boys and girls were friendly. It was very easy to make "friends" with the opposite sex. The Archaeologist chatted up a married woman and took her back to sleep at our place.

One night I was rather bored at a club and my friend Jack said, "I'll take care of it!" He called a cab that took us to an infamous area of Krakow. "Where are we going?" I asked him. "It's a surprise", he replied.

We ended up in a ramshackle bordello full of ugly, scantily dressed girls. I told him that this was not for me. I went back down the stairs to the cab driver who was waiting in the street and went home.

Jack and I also went to Poland, to a place near Warsaw, for my friend Bobo's wedding. I remember it as one of the most beautiful and enjoyable weddings I've ever been to.

## Mykonos

It was during our summer break, on June 1, 2011, that my brother, Jack, and my friend Michele (not the Archaeologist, but our business partner) decided to go have some fun clubbing in Mykonos. We rented a rickety car to get around the island more easily. It's a place with a truly incredible sea and scenery, as well as being a popular place for clubs.

We stayed in a nice little house and we also went dancing in the afternoon at parties on the beach.

One day we rented quad bikes and met two girls from the USA, Annie and Stephanie, who we are still in touch with. On subsequent trips to the States, Annie has always been a great help.

I remember one night when we had had our fair share of drinks, and probably very annoying, we went onto the patio to chat up some foreign girls. Later on, we had great fun in a club called the "Scandinavian Pub", a name that guaranteed you'd have a good time!

The day we had to return to Italy, Michele was still so tipsy from the night before that he struggled to get his luggage onto the plane.

## Cuba, the Bahamas, and Miami Beach

Now let me tell you about what we commonly refer to as "the journey of our lives". A three-week, three-destination trip to Cuba, the Bahamas, and Miami Beach in the company of my brother, Jack, my friend Francesco, and his friend Tommaso.

It was the summer of 2012. At one point we even had doubts about whether we should go, as there had been an outbreak of cholera, and parts of Cuba had been badly affected. Everyone was quick to give us advice such as "avoid cocktails with ice, they are very dangerous", and "only drink bottled water". The first night in Havana we fell in with a shady guy who took us to a bar, sat us down, sent a prostitute over to the table and brought us some Cuba Libres full of ice. Perfect: a baptism of fire!

We stayed in Havana for a few days and rented a rickety Chinese car, a blue Geely, to get around. We were stopped on the street by fake soldiers who tried to hitch a ride from us and asked us for money.

We finally arrived, not without some difficulty, in Pinar del Rio. The province of Pinar del Río has 730,626 inhabitants and covers an area of 10,904.03 km². Its capital is the city Pinar del Río. Viñales, a town famous for its beautiful setting, is located in the valley. The most notable feature of the valley is the Mogotes, small hills that stand out from the surrounding plains. There is also a large contemporary rock painting, the Mural de la Prehistoria, which is reminiscent of prehistoric cave paintings. In the same area there are traditional cottages that have no electric light or other modern amenities. There are numerous underground caves; an underground river flows through one of these, the Cueva del Indio, and it can be visited by boat on a guided tour. Tourism drives the economy of this area and relieves it of some of the serious problems suffered in other parts of Cuba. This contributes to making most of the inhabitants of Viñales supporters of Fidel Castro and his politics (Source: Wikipedia).

We slept in a house owned by a local woman that our friend Jack had found. The house was falling apart. There were exposed electrical wires in the bathroom and a pig pen full of pigs in the garden. The woman was very kind to us. She made us mojitos with mint from her garden and sometimes invited us to eat lobster, a traditional and inexpensive dish in the area.

Strangers came knocking on our door. They knew we were foreigners from our car's license plate, and they did everything they could to get money out of us.

We went on some excursions to see the murals in Viñales and visit the premises of a prestigious local company that specialized in the production of Cuban cigars. We continued our trip to the city of Trinidad.

One day, we hired a horse and a guide to visit the region's spectacular waterfalls. Trinidad is a city with about 75,000 inhabitants in the central province of Sancti Spíritus. Together with the nearby Valle de los Ingenios, it has been a UNESCO World Heritage Site since 1988 (Source: Wikipedia).

That day at the waterfalls I ran into someone that I knew from Rome; what a small world! After Trinidad it was time to sample a bit of the "good life" in the more touristy town of Varadero.

Varadero (which means "the place from which boats are launched") is a popular tourist resort on the northern coast of the province of Matanzas and has one of the largest beaches in the Caribbean. The tour operators also call it Playa Azul, "Blue Beach". Of Varadero the Cubans say "no es Cuba, son los Estados Unidos! ("it is not Cuba, it is the United States!") because of the extremely touristy nature of the place (Source: Wikipedia).

We had a nice room. Chickens freely wandered the streets (to give you an idea of the place). I took my friend Jack to a local clinic as he was convinced that he had caught cholera. I was shocked: it was the dirtiest clinic I have ever seen in my life. Jack had several tests carried out but, fortunately, it was just gastritis and not cholera.

We went out with some girls that we met in Varadero. Jack's girl had a young son, while my girl was a bit younger. They were our guides on trips and accompanied us to the club, but they were extremely poor. One day we went to pick them up at their house and found out that they didn't even have running water at home.

We went back to Havana at the end of the trip and one evening we arranged, with some locals, to attend the famous carnival.

My brother and Tommaso had a bad stomachache after dinner, so they went home. My friend Francesco and I went to a club with some locals.

They let us into the club ahead of the everyone else, almost as if we were a couple of stars. I remember that two Cuban girls latched on to us. At one point while dancing, Francesco told me: "I have a stomachache, I'm going to the bathroom for a moment". He found a bathroom with doors that wouldn't lock, a bodyguard outside, and no toilet paper.

He told me that he cleaned up as best as he could before coming back to dance with us. A girl took his hand and started kissing it; how disgusting! I think this is my favorite story from the vacation.

The next day my girl suggested I go to her house. I was a bit worried, because it was frowned upon to be seen going to a girl's house. I took a cab and was driven to the outskirts of Havana. She introduced me to her aunt, who was a lovely lady, and then we went off to another room.

The second major stop on the trip was the Bahamas, more precisely the capital Nassau. We stayed in a "pimps" residence with a massive casino, and we played a bit on the slots.

Then we went to Paradise Beach, one of the most beautiful beaches in the world, and rented jet skis. In the Bahamas I remember that we ate some really unpleasant and questionable food, while in Cuba they had a much healthier diet.

The last stop on our trip was Miami Beach. Luckily we have a friend who lives there, Annie, who showed us all the best places to go.

## Amsterdam

In March 2013 I went to Amsterdam for a few days with my former partner.

It was on that vacation that I discovered the Wagamama food chain, a restaurant serving Asian food inspired by Japanese cuisine. I remember a jumble of bikes, parked and riding around, sex shops, and buying a joint from a bar and smoking it in a park in the center of Amsterdam.

## Thailand

It was July-August 2013 when my former partner Silvia and I decided to take a trip, one that was definitely out of the ordinary, to Thailand.

We flew from Milan to Bangkok and stayed in a beautiful hotel near the Chao Praya, one of the main rivers in Thailand. On the first day Silvia didn't feel well, maybe because of the long flight. I went out in the evening to explore a local supermarket to grab a bite to eat.

To get around the city we often used a tuk-tuk, or a rickshaw, which is the typical means of transport in Asia for short trips (They used pick-up trucks for longer journeys).

We went out to enjoy Thai food and drink mojitos at a rooftop bar, a skyscraper restaurant, with a former Italian colleague of Silvia's, which was a unique experience. The next day we went to a local market and I still remember the strong smell of fish.

One of the best experiences you can have in Thailand is eating pad thai on the street, which is a traditional Thai street food made of rice noodles sautéed in a wok with shrimp, meat, or tofu, along with vegetables, peanuts, spices, and tasty condiments such as tamarind juice or fish sauce (Source: Giallozafferano).

We visited the beautiful temples of Chiang Mai by bike and one day we visited the local zoo. There were all kinds of animals, including pandas, bears, and hippopotamuses; an experience not to be missed if you love animals.

One day we went to eat in an outdoor restaurant on the river, which I had chosen thinking it would be romantic. Unfortunately the food was terrible, and we saw some kind of pink snails attached to the pier. It was a really disgusting place. In the evening and the next day, we both had fevers and stomachaches. We often ate take-away food from the stalls, especially at lunchtime. I was particularly fond of corn on the cob.

The second stop was in a beautiful hotel near the sea in the tourist town Koh Samui. To get downtown we mainly used pick-up trucks and the journey was an adventure in itself. Koh Samui is very touristy and it is not uncommon to hear people speaking Italian.

The last stop in Thailand was the island of Koh Tao, quieter and less messy than Koh Samui. We had an apartment in the middle of the jungle, which was a great adventure and a lot of fun. We often had geckos visit in the evening.

I had rented a decrepit 50 cc scooter that we rode around on like crazy people.

One day I remember going with Silvia to one of the more remote beaches in Koh Tao. We saw a lizard on the road, and we had to navigate a long, dirt path.

On the way back we couldn't get the scooter up to the dirt road, so I made Silvia get off and tried to go alone. However, my sandals broke (never drive without shoes) and I went careening down to the shore on the scooter, a really uncomfortable ride, and I had to pay a deposit for the damage I'd done to it.

**Greece**

In the summer of 2014, my ex and I decided to go to Greece. We planned to rent a car and visit the Chalkidiki peninsula, in the southeast Balkans. The peninsulacovers an area of about 4,400 km² and juts out into the northern Aegean Sea in a southeastern direction, between the Gulf of Thessaloniki in the west and the Gulf of Orfani in the east (Source: Wikipedia).

The area is famous for the three beautiful peninsulas of Cassandra, Sitonia and Mount Athos.

For the first part of the vacation, we stayed in Porto Koufo in Sitonia, the largest natural harbor in Greece. We often went down to Toroni beach to snorkel. The beach is also famous for its many restaurants strung along the coast. One day we took a trip to the famous Kalabaka Meteora, an important center in the north of Greece, a popular tourist destination, and a UNESCO World Heritage Site.

Meteora (which means "suspended in the air") is an area with numerous natural rock towers. Monasteries have been built (also called "meteora") on several of these towers, which are famous for their breathtaking locations perched as they are at the top of sheer cliffs. Today there are six monasteries still in use (Agios Stefanos, Agia Triada, Gran Meteora, Varlaam, Roussanou and Agios Nikolaos), and a seventh that is uninhabited. Others have been destroyed and some of the ruins can still be seen.

Until the last century the monasteries could only be reached by ladder or using pulley systems. Now there are stairs in the masonry or carved into the rock, which are tricky to navigate but not too tiring to climb, usually taking about ten minutes. Tourists can visit some parts of the monasteries, such as the church, and the largest one has a museum.

The panorama is quite suggestive. Foreigners have to pay a fee to enter the monasteries and there are towels available for women to wear like a skirt to cover bare legs.

The morphology of the place and the towers are the result of sandstone erosion. Most probably, the erosion began around 25 million years ago, caused by a river delta that flowed into the sea over what is now the plain of Thessaly. Then the land was shaped by water and wind, leading to the formation of four groups of towers that stand up to 400 meters tall. Thanks to its unique rocky formations, Meteora is now a popular destination for climbers from all over the world (Source: Wikipedia).

We then stayed in Afytos for several days, also known as Athitos, a hill town with stone houses and paved streets overlooking the Gulf of Toroneos and the famous beaches at the bottom of the cliff.

The main square is dominated by the church of Agios Dimitrios, dating back to the 19th century. Macedonian restaurants and bars with a sea view are dotted along the coast and the cliffs. The Folklore Museum preserves ceramics, textiles, and works of art. The Afytos Festival is held in the summer, during which you can admire street art and listen to live music (Source: Google).

**Milan**

Here is a brief note about Milan, the city where I used to live.

In March 2015, I took my ex to Carlo Cracco's restaurant and asked her to get engaged with me. I spent a lot of money that night on dinner and the ring: an unforgettable evening.

## Sardinia

It was the summer of 2015 when I went to Sardinia with Silvia, my brother, and his partner. Our first stop was Costa Rei, where we stayed in Casa Pitzus, which had also become a famous WhatsApp group.

Sardinia has some of the most beautiful beaches in the world (and I've traveled a lot). You can eat well there and it's definitely a place where I'd like to live, especially in summer. It was a vacation full of the sea, inland farmhouses, and the coast, and we rented a car to get around.

We traveled to the south coast, then on to the green coast where I saw the most beautiful beach and sea view of my life, at Cala Domestica. On the southwest coast of Sardinia, on the borders of Sulcis, is the beautiful bay of Cala Domestica, framed by high cliffs and dominated by a Spanish tower. It's a place where mining history and wild nature merge into a single scene (Source: Regione Sardegna).

## Japan

The chosen destination for our 2015 winter vacation was Japan. We took a direct flight from Milan that took around 12 hours. The first stop was the capital, Tokyo, a metropolis of over 13 million inhabitants. We used the super-efficient subway to get around. Tokyo is a city with a large number of restaurants, games stores, and brightly illuminated mega buildings.

In Japan they are famous for healthy food, especially sushi, but they also have some exceptionally good meat dishes that I will talk about later.

When in Tokyo be sure to visit the different neighborhoods, each of which has its own unique characteristics and peculiarities. Ginza is the most famous business district in Japan, but it's also where you can find the Imperial Palace.

Rather than a neighborhood, I remember Akihabara as one huge electronics supermarket. Here you can buy a range of items from small and original gadgets to extremely sophisticated devices.

As in most markets, a purchase is usually preceded by some intense negotiations. Akihabara is also a sort of technology museum: it is possible to find still-working versions of the first PCs, as well as mechanical robots from the eighties. (Source: Dreaming of Japan).

Then we went to the district of Shibuya, without doubt one of the most dynamic and well-known areas of the city. The neighborhood is illuminated by huge screens on all the buildings in the area, and there is a wide variety of stores (especially clothing and music), restaurants and love hotels.

The young people of Shibuya express themselves through the art of cosplay and ganguro fashion, making the neighborhood even more colorful and unique.

I must also mention Ikebukuro, a popular neighborhood famous for its "Maiden Road" (Otodome Rodo), a name which refers to a major shopping and cultural center for anime and manga targeted to women. Sunshine City is a must-see for those who visit this fascinating district (Source: Dreaming of Japan).

We spent New Year's Eve in Tokyo. There was a large, illuminated tower and an imposing bonfire to celebrate the New Year. After Tokyo, the next stops were Osaka (a very touristy city), Kyoto with its splendid museums, a city not to be missed that expresses the true essence of Japan, and Takayama, a traditional mountain town.

One day we visited Nara Park, famous for its wild deer. According to local folklore, the deer from this area were considered to be sacred after they were visited by Takemikazuchi-no-mikoto, one of the four gods of the Kasuga Shrine. He was said to have been invited by Kashima (in the Ibaraki Prefecture) and appeared on Mount Mikasa riding a white deer. From that time onward, the deer were considered divine and sacred by both the Kasuga Shrine and Kōfuku-ji.

Killing one of these sacred deer was a crime punishable by death until 1637. After the Second World War the deer were officially stripped of their sacred/divine status and were instead designated as a "national treasure" and protected as such (Source: Wikipedia). I didn't really like Osaka. It was very touristy and commercial, but I remember liking Kyoto and Fushimi Inari a lot.

Fushimi Inari and the surrounding area are important not only for the shrine of the same name, but also for the walkway that leads from the temple into the forest that surrounds it: a tunnel made from thousands of red torii (gates) (Source: Dreaming of Japan).

In Takayama we stayed in a beautiful place near a river, with its own a spa, which we certainly did not hesitate to make use of. We also went to a restaurant to eat the delicious and expensive local meat.

We then went back to Tokyo and visited the Tokyo Sky Tree, which left a deep impression on me. It is a telecommunications tower with a panoramic view located in Sumida, a district of Tokyo. It became the tallest structure in Japan in 2010 and, when completed in 2012, it became the tallest free-standing tower in the world and the second tallest artificial structure in the world at 634 meters, second only to the Burj Khalifa skyscraper in Dubai (Source: Wikipedia).

**Apulia**

Summer 2016 was the turn of Apulia, and I don't think I've ever eaten so well during any other vacation. With both meat and fish available at a good price and its town festivals, Apulia is definitely one of my favorite places to stay.

Among the top restaurants we ate at, I especially remember "Il Trabucco", which had a sea view, and another wonderful view from the town of Polignano a Mare.

One evening we went with the friends we were vacationing with to eat meat in a local restaurant. It was a butcher's shop where you could choose your favorite cut of meat at the counter, they would cook it in front of you and then you'd eat it on a terrace outside. All very pleasant, but it was a pity that we all suffered from severe stomachaches after dinner. Perhaps the meat was not very fresh.

I fondly remember Sagra di Maglie, a city in Lecce, where I tried a traditional pasticciotto, and the city of Alberobello where we slept in a trullo (a traditional Apulian dry stone hut with a conical roof).

We also visited Matera with a guide. I think it's the most beautiful city in the world, and I whole-heartily recommend it.

**New York**

I end my travel review from "One Thousand and One Nights" with New York, which we visited in December 2016.

There's a reason why New York is one of the most popular cities in the world to visit, especially during the Christmas holidays: Central Park becomes a large skating rink where people can rent ice skates and soak up the local atmosphere.

There is certainly no lack of opportunities for shopping and I happily recall a dinner we had in a restaurant inside the train station, recommended by a friend.

We also couldn't miss the Brooklyn Bridge and a boat trip to the Statue of Liberty. We then went home and took it easy, partly because Silvia was expecting our little girl, Amelia.

# Chapter 3:
# Work and Unemployment

Now that I've told you about my education and hobbies, let's move on to my work life.

While at university, I started working weekends as a seating attendant in San Siro Stadium. I was stationed at a ramp in the stadium and I had to check everyone trying to enter to make sure that they had the right ticket.

This was easier said than done when you were confronted by a crowd of Milan Ultràs (an enthusiastic group of fans, to say the least) trying to come up the ramp. It was better to avoid them or stall them until you had the backup of a bodyguard, whose job was to keep order during games. I saw a lot of punches thrown and one of my co-workers was even threatened with a knife once. Those people were no joke.

The nice thing was that the company I worked for paid you a little bit and gave you the opportunity to watch the second half of the game for free, when fans had stopped coming up the ramp and had taken their places.

I worked there for several years, and I was always aware that it was an extremely dangerous job. My bosses intentionally seemed to place me at "red" sections, which were those most coveted by the Ultràs, who had usually paid for the cheaper "blue" sections.

Although I was rather good at negotiations, my skills were not enough to deal with those people. I had to think of another ruse to give myself some peace of mind.

I came up with the idea of printing some signs that said: "The ramps are monitored by surveillance cameras. Offenders will be identified and prosecuted". I stuck some of these fake signs on my ramp and they proved to be an excellent deterrent. Not only that, but I even managed to come across as a friend of the Ultràs'. I would say, "Are you sure you want to come through here!? The signs say that they've installed an identification system with cameras. I wouldn't want you to get into trouble". The usual response was, "Thanks, pal. I hadn't realized these assholes had put in cameras".

I had one year left before finishing my marketing degree and I got an internship as Junior Product Manager for an important Italian publisher.

I had to pass three interviews to get the job. In the second one I was particularly impressed by my supervisor, Maurizio, who looked at my resume and said: "You write music on a computer!? Of the hobbies listed on my resume, I mentioned that I had been producing songs on the computer with my brother. He didn't care so much about my language skills or my work ambitions. I think my hobby convinced him that I was a creative person.

So I got the job. I was working for men's magazines, covering topics such as cars, travel, and computer science. I was able to work with some fantastic people, both managers like my boss, Maurizio, and my supervisor Francesco Paolo, and the editors-in-chiefs of the various newspapers.

I especially remember the friendships, projects, and good-natured arguments with Alessandro (the car magazine editor), Giorgio (the computer magazine editor), Giancarlo (a dynamic boss, an all-rounder, and a great fan of travel) and Giorgio (the former Editor-in-Chief of a popular weekly news magazine). I had a very friendly relationship with my colleagues Francesco, Massimiliano, and Matteo, and with the journalist Andrea, and I always had a lot of respect for the managers Carlo and later Ernesto, Carlo, Andrea, and Roberto. It is not an easy task to run a large publishing firm.

I can't deny that it was very difficult at times. I worked hard, while simultaneously studying at night in order to finish my exams. I got very tired and inevitably my grade point average dropped, and I didn't go out at all, to save money.

After adding another six months to my internship, my boss called me into his office and reluctantly told me that, due to the economic crisis that had hit the publishing sector particularly hard, he could not renew my contract. My world collapsed in on me.

Although I had always done my best in my studies and at work, I suddenly found myself unemployed. I had to return home after all the sacrifices, especially financial, that my parents had made for me. I began to look for work, mainly on the Internet and on specialized websites.

I got an offer from a family-run plastics company near my own town. My boss was a rather histrionic woman who had a thousand-and-one ideas and told me that she had a plan to start a business to import biodegradable toothbrushes that she had seen in China.

I accepted the job and, armed with some sample toothbrushes, I went from store to store to try to sell them. I liked the concept, and the fact that the brushes were environmentally friendly, but it was a really flimsy product. I remember it would break if you shook it hard in your hand. I couldn't bring myself to sell a product like that to people, so I quit.

Fortunately, six months later the head of the publishing company called me and told me they were looking for someone to develop the company's online men's magazine business. I couldn't believe my ear: it was my dream job. I had even written my thesis on the integration of paper and the web in the tourism and travel sector. I happily accepted and together with my fantastic co-workers Floria, Claudio, Marco, Junio and Francesco, I developed a new car website.

Many other projects followed with advertising agencies, journalists, web editors of various sites, and with customers in the automotive and other sectors.

One day I drove past a driving school. It was pouring rain and I saw some kids with umbrellas about to take their written exam and I thought: "Why do they have to go to driving school in this weather?" That's when I got the idea to offer learners a free online service for the written exam for driver's licenses.

I was already an SEO fanatic, making sure keywords placed high up in search engine results. I read books on the industry and motivational books such as "The Great Trilogy" by O.G. Mandino, "Rich Dad Poor Dad" by Robert T. Kiyosaki, "Warrent Buffet and the Interpretation of Financial Statements " by Mary Buffet and David Clark, and "The 4-Hour Workweek" by Timothy Ferris.

After years as an employee, I wanted to achieve my dream of becoming my own boss. I really liked the idea of being able to manage my own time. Having time at your disposal means that you can spend more of it with your loved ones, or with your partner, and have more opportunities to cultivate your hobbies.

I had time to take my little girl Amelia to the park near our home almost every morning, something that many other dads can't do because they are at work. Trust me, seeing your little girl taking her first steps in the grass is a feeling that money can't buy.

I have always thought of myself as the dynamic type, and for this reason over the years we have diversified our sites and our business a great deal.

My goal is to help my loved ones and my friends do rewarding work, transforming a hobby into a job if possible. In my opinion, this is the key to business success and a strategy that would help combat some of the problems in the Italian economy.

We have been collaborating with a large advertising agency since 2016.

As well as private cars, we have built up a network for commercial and industrial vehicles, a site dedicated to luxury cars, and we certainly have no shortage of ideas for the future.

Seven people currently work for the company and we aim to increase the number of employees over the coming years.

This type of work leaves me with a lot of free time. Every now and then I go for a walk, go pick mushrooms, play table tennis with my father, or simply go to the village bar on my own for an aperitif.

Of course, I have never forgotten my humble origins or the financial sacrifices my parents made to raise me and pay for my studies, so I get angry with those who are overly pessimistic, those who think only of themselves, those who never change their minds or apologize, those who don't respect the deadlines and regulations of the working world, which remains one of the most precious things we have, especially in these difficult times.

# Chapter 4:

# Romance and Amelia

In the course of my life, I have had three love affairs that were important to me.

The first one was with a girl from the province of Milan, four years younger than me, who always visited my region on vacation. Our romance lasted six years, with its ups and downs, until I started university.

Then I was with a fellow university student for about ten months. Then I met, at work, the girl who would become the mother of my daughter Amelia, the most important person in my world.

I was with her for several years until, for various reasons, our love story came to an end, but I will always respect her and hold her in high regard, even if sometimes it seems as if I feel the exact opposite.

Like me, my ex shares a passion for travel, nature, work, food, sports, and culture, and I believe she will be a great teacher for our daughter.

As you may have noticed, I can't stop talking about my daughter Amelia, who has always been an inspiration to me. I decided to live my life for her, to spend more time with her and share as many experiences with her as possible.

I have a fond memory of taking her in her stroller to Porta Venezia Park in Milan. I also set up an email address for her, which I write to in order to record her progress over the months and send her photos I take on my smartphone.

On January 4, 2019, when I was sure I wouldn't make it through chemotherapy, described in more detail in a later paragraph, I wrote her a letter that I've added in its entirety below.

"My dearest child, I would have loved the joy of watching you grow, of protecting you from the blows of everyday life, giving you strength and passing on my values, of sharing your enthusiasm in every new discovery you make.

However, as is often said, it is not the quantity, but the quality of time spent together that is important, and the moments we have spent together, although certainly too few, are the most precious moments of my life.

During your first year of life we had a symbiotic relationship. My job allowed me to work flexible hours and every minute of my free time was dedicated to you.

You loved to go to Porta Venezia Park to play on the swing, or to Gam (a children's park) where you took your first steps in the grass.

Not that we didn't have fun at home; on the contrary, without being aware of the passage of time, we would spend hours building things, drawing, and playing hide-and-seek; how you loved hunting me down! You would call out "Peek a boo Daddy" and I'd hide behind the door and like a little robot you'd come looking for me. And when you found me, we'd laugh together.

When it was time for your afternoon nap, we'd take your stuffed animals, lie down together in a big hug and fall asleep. Every once in a while I'd sleep next to you in the afternoon and it was such a precious moment. This was the self-fulfillment of a father who loved to take care of his little girl from breakfast in the morning, who played games with her, fed her, changed her diapers, and put her to bed.

I can't pretend that it wasn't demanding. During the day, all my attention was focused on you and I had to work at night to catch up, but I would do the same again because I knew that those moments were unrepeatable. Every day with you was new, and I was proud to be by your side as you took your first steps in the world.

We went to the seaside, to the lake, and you, your mother and I went up, you in your backpack, to a mountain hut 2,000 meters above sea level. We never slowed down and tried to enjoy every moment because life is unpredictable.

You are still much too young to remember me, but I hope the photos and videos you have will be some consolation. I have given all the passwords you'll need to Uncle Marco. I also created an email in your name where I've recorded, step by step, the first five months of your life. I hope that one day you will want to read these messages, but if not, I understand.

Maybe you'll be curious to know who your dad was, so I'll try to tell you and pass on my values.

**Childhood**

I spent my childhood in the hills of Ameno, a place I remained deeply attached to. The view of Monte Rosa across Lake Orta was always enough to put my mind at ease. When I was a child there were no cell phones, no electronic devices, so I spent my free time in the fresh air, kicking a ball around or following streams like an explorer.

Grandmother Caterina worked close to home and often took me to her office. Grandfather Renato worked a little further away and I used to see him in the evenings and on weekends. I remember waiting for him, anxiously looking out of the window. This was also because he used to bring me stickers for my Panini album.

I was lucky enough to have great parents, the best I could have wished for. They were always there for me, no matter what. They always made sacrifices to give me the opportunity to go to the beach, travel, and study in the best schools, even if it meant that they constantly had to tighten their belts. Your grandmother was a clerk, your grandfather a manual laborer, so we certainly didn't live the high life.

When I was seven years old, I asked them to give me the greatest gift of my life... a little brother!

## My brother

And then my little brother arrived. Although it was well before your grandmother's due date, Uncle Marco was born. And in hindsight, I can confirm that it was the best gift they could have given me, which makes me really sorry that I didn't have time to give you such a great gift.

We were two very different people, but we would have done anything for one another. It was fantastic to have someone I could trust unconditionally, a shoulder to cry on, but also someone to share the fun times with, and together we had many.

## Adolescence

Although as a child I was a cherub, from the age of 13 to 18 I have to say that I gave my saintly parents a hard time. Conflicts arose and at times I felt like my parents were against me. I don't realize that the advice they gave and the restrictions they placed were for my own good.

You'll go through this phase too. I can already predict that you'll make Mama Silvia's hair turn white. Ever since you were a little girl, we knew that you were a tough cookie!

You will have mood swings. You may think that you are ugly (impossible to believe, because you are beautiful, always remember that!), full of flaws, and in conflict with the world, maybe even a little paranoid. For a while, I used to take photos of my hair every day because I was convinced that I was going bald.
And then the first crushes will come, you'll feel butterflies in your stomach. It will be a magical time during which you'll live in the light, have fun, and think you are immortal.

Enjoy it all, my little one. Respect your body and study hard, for a good education is essential for making your way in life. Listen to your mom, even if you sometimes feel like she comes from another planet. She has also gone through this phase, so she'll understand what you are going through and give you sound advice.

After every disappointment, remember this saying that Nonna Caterina used to always say to me: "As one door closes, another door opens". She would always say this to me at the end of a romance, a friendship, or after a failure at school or at work.

At the time, I thought it was just a saying to make me feel better, but as the days went by it became more and more meaningful. It was true, roads were opening up before me, perspectives that in my previous state of mind I could not see, and every time it was like a breath of pure oxygen, with new horizons to discover.

I went to middle school in Orta San Giulio, in an old building with a view over the lake. I really liked that environment, but not so much the studying. What gave me an edge, at school, in sports, at work, was my positive, competitive spirit. It always bothered me to "lose", to look bad, so even if I didn't really feel like it, I studied hard so I would be among the best.

It's a form of self-respect; doing things well builds your self-confidence and makes you feel better about yourself and others. I hope that I have passed this aspect of my character on to you. It will help you do well in life and fully commit to the paths you choose to take.

In the meantime, I had also started to cultivate a passion that I had had since a child: soccer. From the age of 13 to 19 I played for the Bolzano Novarese and San Maurizio teams. I was a forward, so I loved to score goals. We were not a great team, but I had a lot of fun. Nonno Tozzi came with me to games. He never missed one, and it made me really happy to score goals while I knew he was watching.

I hope you play some sports too: it strengthens your body and spirit. If you are part of a team, all the better. You will learn to help each other to achieve a common goal, and you'll discover what it means to lose and tp share the joy of victory.

I attended the Scientific High School in Borgomanero, which I remember as being among the happiest and most enjoyable years of my life. I left with a good grade, 98/100, and had met people who became some of my best friends. Years later I was still in touch with them. I started that school as a kid and came out more mature, although I think I only really achieved full maturity when I began to live alone during my university studies.

**University**

After high school I really didn't really know which way to go. I wanted to continue studying, but where?

My ambition led me to take an entrance exam for one of the most renowned universities in Italy, Bocconi in Milan. There were so many at the exam, students from all over Italy, and I, like 900 others, had chosen the CLEACC course, Economy and Management for Culture, the Arts and Information. There were only 320 spots and your dad was among those selected! It was a great thrill for my parents and me.

I had a scholarship, but the course was still very expensive. My parents were fantastic and supported me financially so I could enroll and study in Milan. I lived in a lot of very different areas; first in Bonola in public housing, then in Via Cadore with five roommates (absolute chaos), then in Piazzale Lodi with Uncle Marco and two other roommates, and finally in Piazzale Gorini with your Uncle Marco and another roommate, in what was undoubtedly the best house of them all.

Apart from the first year, I didn't mess around much during university. The course was quite hard and I had a strong sense of duty to my parents who were supporting me. I couldn't afford to go off the rails.

In the first year I had a nine month-long relationship with a girl in my course and in the second year I started a long relationship with a girl I had met at the lake, which lasted six years, years fraught with many ups and downs. I thought she was the right person to start something special with, but over time she proved to be fragile and fickle.

Every so often she would have doubts about our relationship, and it made me feel bad. Then she came to realize the value of our relationship and came back to me. In short, it was a real emotional roller-coaster, which I had the courage to bring to an end at the age of 27. I spent two weeks feeling terrible and it took me a few months to get over her completely. Some say that to come to terms with the end of a relationship it takes a period of time proportional to the time you spent together. But in the end, I'm happy I made this decision and Nonna was right once again, one door had closed but another door of opportunity was opening.

When you are at the end of a romance, remember that somewhere out there in the world there is the person who is right for you. The one waiting for me was your mother, who would soon come to the end of one of her own big love stories and meet me.

But let's take a step back. I finished the three years of university on time with a grade of 103/110. I never missed a deadline, so I had a good but not excellent grade average. However, there were subjects that I just could not get into (private law, finance, and languages).

It was time to make more choices. Should I continue the CLEACC program with a specialist subject, or change? I was grasping in the dark, but in my heart, I knew that two more years of that course would not be of much value to me. There was too little real-world application, too much art and culture for my liking. I did not want to end up running a museum.

And so I chose the specialist degree in Marketing Management. We studied how to predict what the market wanted, products, and methods of communication.

After the first two weeks I had an existential crisis. I didn't like my course and I was convinced that I had made all the wrong choices in life. Me, who had always left his choices open by taking "general" courses, had gone on to specialize in marketing.

I talked to a dear friend of mine in my class, who told me to hang in there, that things would get better. And in fact they did. The lessons became more and more interesting, with a lot of group work and real testimonies from real companies. I began to get a glimpse of something more concrete, a foretaste of the world of work.

If from time to time, you feel a bit lost, it could be just a passing phase and you may need to change things up a bit. But if, over time, you realize in your heart that the road you have chosen is the wrong one for you, don't be afraid to take a step back. We only have one life, and it should bring you joy and satisfaction, so do the things that make you feel good.

At the end of the first year, students with a higher grade point average were given a wonderful opportunity: a three-week summer course at UCLA, in Los Angeles. It's not every day you get an offer like that, so I jumped at it. I had already regret not participating in the European study abroad program, for financial and romantic reasons, so that was one more reason to set off!

I liked the courses and managed good average grades. At the beginning of the second year, I found another internship: a large Italian publishing house offered me a job as a Junior Product Manager to handle their car and travel magazines. I was over the moon. I liked the job very much and I threw myself into it body and soul, working until late in the evening. I still had several exams to take and had to study at night. After six months they renewed my internship for another six months. I had to hang in there and finish university. My grades plummeted and it became more and more tiring to work and study at the same time. I struggled on like this for more than a year, drinking coffee in the evenings to keep me awake after a hard day's work, but in the end, I managed to graduate on time. My thesis earned 101/110, which focused on the travel magazine I was managing.

I was happy. I had finished my studies, I was doing a job I liked, and my parents were proud of me. I started to make some money too when, after the internship, they gave me a project contract. But the global economic crisis was fast approaching and it would have an impact on me too.

## Unemployment and rebirth

After two and a half years working in the publishing company, they let me go. My world fell apart. I couldn't continue to pay rent in Milan and so I went back to my parents' house in Ameno.

I was a failure and all my hard work and my parents' sacrifices had gone up in smoke in an instant. Returning to my parents' home after years of independence was an emotional time-bomb waiting to explode. Things were not the same between us.

In May 2009, I went to Ireland for three weeks to improve my English and then went back home to start sending out resumes. During that time I had one-on-one and group interviews, but nothing came of them. There wasn't much work available and the competition was intense. It was one disappointment after another. Time passed and the situation at home became less and less manageable, especially because of my state of mind.

Then one day a bright light came in the middle of the darkness. It was September, I was in my car, it was raining heavily, and I was coming back from Borgomanero when I passed a driving school.
There were some soaking wet boys going to take their written tests and at that moment my first thought was: why do they have to do this? Why can't they take the tests from home? I talked about it with Uncle Marco, a computer genius, and a few months later Patentati.it was born.

I dedicated all my free time teaching myself the techniques to get articles high up on the search engines. Michele, a dear friend of mine who was passionate about cars, was also involved in the project. At that moment I had a hobby, a passion, which would become a real profession years later, a hugely satisfying part of my life, and redemption from the bad luck I had previously had in the world of work.

I like the saying: "Ideas are in the air, you just have to become good at intercepting them and putting them into practice." And also, "You don't necessarily have to do something that is completely original. Sometimes to be successful you just have to take an idea that already exists and execute it better." I don't know if you'll be a good manager, or entrepreneur, or something else.

Since you were a small child, it's been clear that you have something extra, and you must engage it to find your own way. If you don't like what you are doing, change it and try to find a job that brings you genuine satisfaction. Things won't always go your way but doing what you like is an important part of living a happy and fulfilled life.

In the meantime, I also found a part-time job at a plastics firm in the area. They wanted to develop a biodegradable toothbrush and I was supposed to take part in all the market research and development. The owners were odd, quite visionary, but I liked them. However, one day the boss came back from China with some terrible biodegradable toothbrushes (they broke in my hand), took me to lunch and told me: now you are a salesman. It's your job to sell these toothbrushes! I immediately understood that the adventure there was over. I really couldn't bring myself to sell that crap to people, for ethical reasons.

In March 2010, my old boss from the publishing company called me and told me that a position had become available. It was a fixed-term contract with no promise of an extension, but at least there was a real job waiting for me. So I went back for a year to manage the car and computer magazines. But I had learned my lesson. I knew that the job would never be permanent. In the evening I dedicated my time to our project that was growing fast, and then I sent out resumes.

Then, just as they were welcoming me back to the publishing company, with a few months' notice I was offered a job at a leading telecommunications company. It was also a temporary contract. I didn't even like it much as a job but at least I would have avoided the nightmare of being unemployed again.

But life really is a revolving door, and something was about to happen that would deal me another new hand of cards and lead to me meeting my future wife, your mother.

My contract with the publishing company only had a week left. I was getting ready to sign the telecommunications company's contract when my boss called me to a meeting. The company wanted to establish a presence on the web and launch a car website and the boss thought I would be the right man to implement that project. They made me a lucrative financial offer and gave me guarantees about future permanent employment. I was in heaven: a job I liked that was well paid.

At that time, my company was taking on a lot of staff. A new manager was recruited from a multinational telephone company and they brought in some people from their previous company, including my future wife, your mother Silvia.

## Your mother and me

We met in the office in April 2011, crossing paths in the corridor, but didn't work much together, just a monthly meeting where we began to respect each other's work, but nothing more. At that time, your mother was in a relationship with a Sicilian man, but I had just come out of a six-year relationship and I had no intention of throwing myself back into another one right away.

I traveled a lot with my friends during that time, to Barcelona, Edinburgh, Mykonos, Cuba, Miami, and the Bahamas; beautiful memories that I will treasure forever.

In the fall of 2012 things began to change. Mom was easing herself out of her relationship and, without knowing it, I was ready to start a new chapter in my life. Silvia and I began texting each other after a meeting and from then on, we couldn't stop. We spent the evenings texting each other on WhatsApp. After about a month we had our first date, which went very well. I had no doubt that she was the person I had been looking for all my life. I immediately understood that she was a serious, reliable, intelligent woman with all the qualities that would allow us to build something meaningful together.

I had fun with your mom, and we took a lot of trips together to Amsterdam, Thailand, Japan, Sardinia, Apulia and New York, with you in her belly.

We always had a good relationship, although of course we had our ups and downs. But if you love a person, everything always works out.

After a few months I moved in with her even if I had already been spending more time at her place than at mine for a while.

We had a good time living together, and from the very beginning we shared a common outlook on life. We both wanted to build something special together, to have a family. In fact, a few years later the family did expand a little when Braulio the cat, a foundling from the lake, came to live with us.

You were very fond of him too. When you were little he used to sleep beside you and when he moved to the lake with your grandparents you couldn't wait to see him. You called him "Bau-Bau" and were always trying to pull his tail.

But our plan for a family was not limited to just a cat, of course, and in July 2017 you came along, and became the greatest joy of our lives.

It was an exceptionally long delivery, almost 32 hours from the first contractions. Your mother was tenacious and incredibly brave during those hours. At 8.54 a.m. on July 12th I saw you for the first time and I cried like a baby. It was an indescribable feeling of joy after nine months waiting for you, imagining how you would look.

There is nothing that provokes greater emotion than the birth of a child and I hope that, when you feel ready, you can experience that feeling too... and share it with a man with a good head on his shoulders. I recommend it!

**To Sum Up**

From that moment you filled our lives with joy, and I felt fulfilled as a man.

You came along just a few months after I had had the courage to leave a permanent job to dedicate myself to my business, which in the meantime had expanded a great deal. We had nine websites and four employees who worked with Michele, Marco, and me.

There are times in your life when you may think, "If I don't do this, I will regret it forever and I will live with the regret of not having tried". Well, personally, I would have regretted not having a baby and not working on my own projects.

Luckily, thanks to my stubbornness, I managed to achieve both my dreams. I haven't had as much time to enjoy them as I would have liked, but I am aware that I have lived a life worth living.

I have learned that we have to live in the present, not always putting things off until tomorrow, because the future is, unfortunately, uncertain and we never know what it may hold for us. I would like you to be able to appreciate the present and to achieve your dreams without postponing them to some indefinite date in the future. With tenacity, willpower, and sacrifice, nothing is impossible.

You have to face life with your head held high, respect people and demand respect from them. I urge you to work to earn people's respect and don't give in to anyone who tries to put you down. Remember you are tough; you're a Rabozzina ;)

Your dad is proud, thoughtful, tenacious, stubborn, a bit touchy, optimistic, reliable, and sincere in close relationships, while being skeptical and a bit detached towards people he doesn't know or with whom he only has a superficial relationship.

I was shy, especially as a child, but over the years I have tried to work on this aspect of my personality, as it can be a hindrance in life.

And, as I already told you, I don't like losing, not even in a game of cards. I admit that sometimes, when the stakes were high, I can become a bit annoyed, but people really have to try hard to make me angry.

I like to eat well, play sports, listen to music, study the things that interest me, and spend time with my real friends, but I also like to be alone sometimes to reflect and dedicate some time to myself.

I prefer not to talk about the time I was ill. I just want you to know that every time I was feeling down, I looked at your photos and videos to pick me up and you gave me the strength to fight on. But you know, in these situations you also need a large dose of good luck.

# Chapter 5:

# Sickness and How To Face It

Now that I had my daughter, I was one of the happiest people in the world, but I couldn't foresee the hard time that fate had in store for me.

It was towards the end of August 2018, when I was 35 years old. One afternoon I went for a walk to pick mushrooms in the woods of Valtellina. When I got home, I realized that I had my neck was swollen.

I hoped that it was just an insect bite but to make sure I immediately booked an ultrasound scan of my neck in a clinic near my home in Milan. After the ultrasound picked up something suspicious, they told me to see a professional hematologist immediately. I chose IEO because in the past the doctors there had been very good with my previous partner's mother.

The hematologist immediately arranged for a biopsy to be carried out on my neck and entrusted me to a colleague who explained the process I was going to go through. I knew it would not be a walk in the park, but I never expected the nightmare that unfolded in the following months.

The biopsy and a subsequent CT scan confirmed there was a tumor, a follicular lymphoma, so doctors decided to destroy the lump with six sessions of a chemo-immunotherapy called R-CHOP. In addition to the four classic drugs cyclophosphamide, adriamycin, vincristine and prednisone, they also decided to use a newer monoclonal drug called Rituximab, to reduce the risk of recurrence.

First a nurse inserted the PICC line. What is a PICC line!? A PICC line is a peripherally inserted central catheter used to inject the chemotherapy drugs and carry out the continuous blood tests that are required. I managed to find a fashionable PICC-cover on the Internet, but it wasn't easy to live with a permanent catheter in your arm for more than six months.

Before starting the chemotherapy in November, I met with my consultant and asked him a thousand questions. I wanted to know everything I could that would help me survive, and the knowledge of what was in store for me and the side effects I could suffer could only make me more prepared.

I asked him questions about the prescriptions and tests I needed; the side effects of chemo, his opinion on Rituximab, the role of vitamin D, and how to improve my blood levels, his thoughts on some alternative medicines, and on any diet I should follow and exercise I should get before and during chemo.

I started the first cycle of chemo-immunotherapy at the beginning of November. I don't remember now if my parents or my brother were with me. They have always been there for me in times of need. I remember a waiting room full of people like me, including some young ones, who were there for chemo.

They called me and I entered a room where another person was already waiting. A nurse explained the whole process to me, and the doses of medicine proportionate to my body weight. She took the bags with the liquid and attached them one by one to the PICC. After the first session, I immediately realized that it would be more difficult than I had anticipated.

Every week after the session I had to have a blood test because my white blood cell count was dropping, which meant I was at greater risk of infection and had to isolate myself as much as possible. If your white blood cells dropped too much, you had to take a shot of a substance called Zartium in your stomach (often self-administered), which cost about 90 euros per syringe. Zartium is a tough drug. It raises your white blood cell count and boosts your immune system but often causes fever and back pain.

I have always used alternative medicine and methods to help me win the battle with cancer. I knew that everything would contribute: chemo, nutrition, sports, homeopathy, alternative medicines, and herbs.

One day I went to Bologna to see Dr. Giuseppe Di Bella. I was very curious about his success in the treatment of tumors in the past. I took inspiration from his ideas and bought some natural drugs at a pharmacy in Bologna that he recommended: Retinoids, vitamin C, vitamin D, and melatonin.

I also bought an Aloe Arborescens, a miraculous medical plant for tumors according to Father Zago and made a smoothie from its leaves following a recipe suggested by the father, mixing in aloe vera, a little honey, and a little grappa.

I paid a lot of attention to good nutrition. I tried to eat organic products as much as possible and I got some exercise when I felt up to it.

Another important suggestion for those who are unfortunate enough to have to undergo chemotherapy is to fast as much as possible before the injection. Fasting has been shown to reduce side effects and improve the effectiveness of chemo.

I have always been interested in the revolutionary Mima Digiuno Diet by Valter Longo, a very influential Italian scientist and one of the world's leading experts on alternative treatments for cancer. I bought one of his books, which was very interesting.

Another piece of advice to help deal with treatment: be confident, curious, and stay open-minded. Use all the weapons you have at your disposal. You must, of course, follow the advice of the doctors, but they don't know everything, and it's your body, after all.

One day the doctors told me a PET scan had shown a spot on my liver. They thought it was a liver metastasis, and I was devastated. But then I asked myself: "How can a tumor move from the neck to the liver in such a short time? I immediately called the uncle of a friend of mine, a great doctor and world-famous professor, and asked for his opinion.

He reassured me by telling me that in his opinion, it was not a metastasis but a liver stain and this proved to be the case, confirmed by a biopsy he suggested I had done.

After each session of chemo I suffered horrendous side effects. I had a fever of 104°F for days and caught bronchopneumonia, which had to be urgently treated with a course of injections.
I spent Christmas 2018 at home with just my parents in order to avoid any infection. They brought me a tray of food and ate alone at the table.

As expected, I lost all my hair, so I wore a hat when out and about. Fortunately, after only three cycles of chemo the lymphoma disappeared, and I was able to avoid another three cycles of therapy that would have had even more severe side effects.

I would like to thank the IEO doctors for their skill and professionalism, and for tolerating a nuisance like me.

Now, fortunately, I'm fine. I'm finishing a cortisone treatment that means that I can't drive, and gives me insomnia, night sweats, and chemically induced hunger (I've gained 15 kg) but compared to chemo it's a piece of cake.

# Chapter 6:

# Financial Freedom and Digital Marketing

The expression financial freedom is used often, especially in motivational books and communications on social networks. But what does financial freedom really mean? I consider it synonymous with free time, with the possibility of spending more time with loved ones and having more time for myself and my interests, without being overly constrained by strict work hours.

I think my work as an entrepreneur is already synonymous with financial freedom. In fact, this offers me the opportunity to work when I like and to dedicate time to my passions without feeling pressured to have to justify a fixed monthly salary, as has been the case in the past.

Then there's the fact of having created something all your own, which gives you an extra boost to work better. Sure I like to unwind and relax, especially during the weekends, but I also enjoy having some free time during the work week.

We founded a media company specialized in the automotive industry, currently with ten owned sites and seven people working for the company full-time.

Our core business is advertising, which we have been managing in     partnership with an important Italian agency since 2016.

We have many ideas for the future, in particular projects in collaboration with major lead generation players, and we are working to create a network of digital driving schools aimed at offering a driving safety guide (not safe driving) for new drivers.

I believe we will succeed, as our ethical and economic motivations are certainly not lacking. My brother, one of my friend's, and I started the company.

We have not always seen things the same, especially when it comes to investments, and this has recently led me to find additional, alternative sources of income. In addition to the classic shares and investments in cryptocurrencies, I have begun to look to crowdfunding some innovative Italian start-ups with high growth potential.

I have purchased shares in four different companies: one specializing in organic pet food, one in online expert consultancy, music-oriented social media, and an e-commerce for vintage items.

Before making each investment, I spoke with the CEOs of the various companies, I asked them about their business model and market growth and expansion strategies. I also offered my availability to collaborate and provide my consultancy in terms of digital marketing.

My main goal is not significant earnings but rather, as I have said, to be able to work when and where I want. Like many other Italians, I would love to live in Barcelona, Spain; I have already laid some foundations to move there, if possible near the sea.

Life is shorter and more unpredictable than we can ever imagine, as my past experiences have taught me. My greatest advice is to never put off your wishes and ambitions for too long, that it's better to take risks.

Those who take risks and make mistakes go further than those who stand still. Last but not least, there's the publication of this book. As I mentioned before, my primary goal is to pass my willpower and positivity on to others. It was my mother who suggested I publish an autobiography, as she experienced the events of my life along with me, step by step.

I certainly wouldn't mind if the book became a bestseller, which is also the main reason why I turned to the publishing services of Bruno Editore. I would like to underline that it was not easy to leave a fixed, full-time job. Before going off on my own, I enjoyed my job working in a large publishing house and I had the opportunity to collaborate with great professionals.

That said, my primary goal was to be able to spend as much time as possible with my young daughter, to take her to the park every morning I could (before she began kindergarten), so having a flexible job was necessary and if I had to make the same choice again I would, a thousand times over.

I have always held networking as an essential aspect of a person's personal and economic growth. In fact, I studied and have been successful in the world of digital marketing, so I am confident when I speak of the field. Instead for other things, especially investments, I prefer to collaborate with people who are more specialized in the fields.

And this is why I have relied on the established skills and knowledge of Bruno Editore for the publication of this book.

**Digital Marketing**

I believe that digitalization opens up great economic possibilities for various people, although it certainly doesn't detract from the importance of always keeping skills up to date and being willing to change things.

I have dedicated my whole life to Digital Marketing, both at work and as a student, and I have always enjoyed applying it to a concrete field such as work.

When I was a student at Bocconi I adored teamwork, working on projects commissioned by real companies. My calling then continued in the workplace, first as an employee and then as an entrepreneur.

I strongly believe in Digital Marketing because it is smart by definition, less bureaucratic and with more practical applications, and also allows an unequalled process of business scalability and internationalization.

When I speak of Digital Marketing, I mean promotion online and on other media, such as social networks, of a company's products, e-commerce, product management and brand reputation, SEO (positioning of keywords on search engines), SEM, and lead generation.

Digital Marketing is applicable to every field, from automotive to pharmaceutical; as I said before, it is a great opportunity to increase your business.

More specifically, I have developed, even self-taught, skills for positioning the right keywords in search engines: an indispensable requirement for those who want to work in online publishing and want to reach a decent number of enthusiasts and users.
In addition to my work which I am highly passionate about, I like to share my advice with other businesses to help them grow.

As I mentioned, my company is specialized in online information dedicated to general cars, premium cars, and commercial and industrial vehicles.

The first site we founded lets youth take unlimited driving license tests online for free. An editorial section about cars was then added to the site, with product presentations, price lists, test drives, and customer press releases.

Then in 2016 we developed a network dedicated to commercial and industrial vehicles: it is a gem, as we are now one of the Italian leaders in online information for this type of vehicle.

We have also recently launched a more niche site dedicated to premium cars and lifestyle. It's not huge, but it satisfies the tastes of many car manufacturers in terms of its placement and target.

**E-commerce and Lead Generation**

One of the most interesting levers of Digital Marketing are e-commerce sites and lead generation. The term e-commerce trivially applies to all online sales, which the period of Covid-19 has clearly accelerated.

As I said before, you can sell almost any product online and make a difference not only in terms of prices, but also service and delivery components, which are increasingly important.

For example, a friend of mine, an artisan specialized in mushrooms, recently sent me a link for an e-commerce site to buy his products.
I was also willing to pay a premium price for his products, but I stopped the purchase when I noticed the extra shipping costs of seven euros for each shipment.

By now people are used to paying little and making good purchases online, so it's important to evaluate every aspect of the supply chain: product quality is not enough anymore.

Amazon has certainly revolutionized the world of online shopping but I am also a fan of the Esselunga home delivery service, where you can comfortably order groceries from home and have them delivered usually within 24/48 hours.

E-commerce is not only revolutionizing the world of products but also of services, which is why I have heavily invested in an Italian start-up that offers professional consultancy online.

In addition to having shares in the company, I have also added my profile as a consultancy expert in Digital Marketing, with no downsides that I can see. I have invested in two other start-ups specialized in e-commerce, one for organic pet food, especially dogs, and another for vintage home furnishings.

Of course, before investing I met their CEOs and asked about their growth prospects, after which I offered my time and advice to collaborate in growing their business.

With our company, we have a focus on those who drive cars and those just getting their driving licenses, so lead generation with offers for new, used, or zero km cars, financing, car and motorcycle insurance, long-term rental, and mobility-related services are all ideal.

The mechanism is quite simple: we define a percentage on leads with the partner (usually estimates in terms of pay per lead) or on the sales of individual products (in this case in terms of pay per sale).

In my opinion, there is great potential for many individuals to turn their passion into their work. In fact, I see on social media, especially Instagram, that there are so many people who are good at cooking, wine, food and regional specialties, passionate about travel, music, books and culture, for which e-commerce or lead generation could be a great way to promote their products and ideas.

As publishers, we don't sell anything but we use lead generation a great deal. As I said, my secret dream is to create a digital network of driving schools and promote driving safety among new drivers (not safe driving).

The issue of safety is of great concern to everyone and many agree that the current driving license exams do not offer our youth the most appropriate tools and knowledge to drive safely on roads.
It is an ambitious project, but with our marketing skills to communicate with many new drivers and with the collaboration of a safe driving instructor, also connected to the association "victims of the road".

Our company currently has lead generation relationships for new cars and financing, but over the next year we intend to greatly expand collaborations.

It is not easy to do business in Italy, as many people are still tied to the idea of a fixed/secure job; unfortunately, there is nothing secure nowadays, especially in the workplace. New technologies offer a great number of opportunities to increase business and improve standard of living, so I urge people to try not to become too fixed to certain ideals.

**SEO and Search Engine Positioning**

The other enormous aspect of Digital Marketing is the positioning of keywords searched by users on search engines. Good positioning and being able to appear on the first page of search engines with certain keywords is certainly a great business card for professionals, agencies or entrepreneurs online, as well as being a great step forward for promoting their products or services.

There are over three billion queries on Google everyday, and about 70% of clicks are on the sites positioned on the first page, with 70% of clicks going to the top five, while the results from sixth to tenth position collect little more than 3%.

Themes such as keyword density, link building, and bounce rate are just some of the factors that determine keyword positioning on search engines.

We are among the top positions with the keyword "driving license quiz" with the first site we developed, and this guarantees we will reach many future new drivers every month.

There is unbridled competition on the names of various car models, which are also very interesting for lead generation and e-commerce business, as well as for communicating with car manufacturers.

As I said, we are lucky enough to work with a large advertising agency and this ensures business continuity from a commercial point of view.

The advertising agency specializes in the sale of banners and special projects. I fondly recall a project for the Maggiora Motor Show with an important car and tire manufacturer.

My partners who are knowledgeable and passionate about cars are invited to product previews by the manufacturers. The international motor shows (Geneva, Paris, Frankfurt) are also a great showcase and a way to forge relationships with car manufacturers, but they were unfortunately canceled in 2020 due to Covid 19.

The manufacturers then leave the new cars available to the press for about two weeks, who write about the new features of the cars and their impressions while driving them, so it is also a lot of work.

As I said, we have put a great deal of effort into product differentiation, and we are one of the market leaders for online information related to commercial and industrial vehicles.

The market is smaller than that of cars, but still counts about 150,000 commercial vehicles and about 40,000 industrial vehicles sold per year (Unrae 2019 data).

The last site we developed, as mentioned, is about premium cars, so luxury, but also accessible. We have emphasized the lifestyle component and everything that lies behind the world of cars. Stories, tales, designers, accessories, and cult locations of cars.

By its very nature, the site does not reach the numbers of a generalist car portal, but has its own clearly defined target audience.

A site that reaches big numbers is not necessarily better, what's important is that it reflects the desires and interests of those who browse it.

The video and photographic component are absolutely essential when you have to sell or sponsor a product. There is often the problem of warehouse costs, but as I said before, these costs are also practically eliminated with lead generation.

We have also explored the path of internationalization, especially on the car side, but at the moment we are more dedicated to the Italian market.

In addition to the automotive sector, we have also thrown ourselves into collateral projects, such as schools and boating, but we have not achieved great results. Social networks are also very important for communicating with your audience.

Tik Tok and Instagram are currently very popular with younger age groups, while Facebook seems to cover a higher age range of the population and Linkedin is more connected to professionals. Twitter, on the other hand, seems to have lost some of its appeal.

There are specific applications excelling in specific fields, such as Spotify for music, Babbel for learning a foreign language, WhatsApp for messaging, not to mention those that let you watch movies and series such as Skygo.

We are certainly ambitious when it comes to further improving as a company, knowing that entrepreneurs must be increasingly "obsessed" with meeting their customers' needs.

What's more, we are not indifferent to ethical issues such as the safety of new drivers, which I have previously mentioned, as well as health and environmental protection. We have various means available for starting dialogues with different people, so we sometimes touch on issues that seem to have little to do with the automotive sector.

We are now a full-fledged Media Company, and we make quality and the pursuit of excellence our strengths. As I already mentioned, various collaborations likely await in the future, as we believe in synergies and in people's skills.

Another goal is to attract talents to work with us, which is why we always carefully evaluate the candidates seeking to work with our company. As I have already mentioned, the digital field has been lucky to have excelled during the worldwide pandemic, unlike many other fields, with the work from home culture already having been encouraged before Covid 19 entered the scene.

This bodes well for the projects and activities planned for the future, without forgetting that although wonderful, it's still a job and it must be respected as such when working with projects and deadlines.

## Leadership and Ethical Work

The topic of leadership has always been dear to me. I have often felt like a leader in my organization, but I have not always been able to behave like an ethical entrepreneur, able to communicate the right things to people.

It really takes very little to pass from being a leader to being a "know-it-all," so it's important to act properly and use correct communication to pursue the common good of the company. I have always tried to improve in this sense, which is also why I often read e-books and listen to the podcasts of a communication agency particularly focused on the topic of leadership.

An e-book I recently read discussed ethical entrepreneurs, so those capable of guiding other people in the organization towards a common good. I very much believe in this definition of a leader as a sort of glue for bringing different people together, to direct individual energies and transform them into a collective workforce.

The same e-book defined a leader as a person who has a higher level of influence on others, a person animated by strong convictions who can stir and animate others to put themselves at the service of the group and be reflected in the leader.

This is easier said than done, especially with people who think very differently from you. I feel like a leader of my company because most of the business diversification ideas have come from me, I personally saw to bringing certain people into projects and making my collaborators work under the best economic and professional conditions.

I don't think I have always been understood by everyone, some may have been offended by my frank approach. I have always worked for the common good, but my communication has not always been flawless.

The author of the book argues that speaking of the common good means concreteness and necessity. The ethical leader understands this concept and puts it into practice in his behavioral choices, encouraging others to do the same for their own good and that of others. Unfortunately, companies and society as a whole have become more accustomed to taking than to giving, thereby subtracting assets, resources, and opportunities.

The importance of correct communication comes to light in this context. Communication that becomes action by fully tracing its etymological origin, "cummunis agere," acting with the other while seeking out a middle ground that is not always agreement but certainly open confrontation aimed at creating a shared good, which creates rather than destroys.

One such example of correct entrepreneurial communication is that of Pope Francis. He always uses a lexicon, common language, to be authentically close to his fellow men and women. A language that comes from the heart rather than from cold rationality and an analytical nature. He is authentically human. He is a concrete example directly contrasting the stereotypical, detached model proposed by some of the vast current literature focusing on leadership.

A basically mechanistic model of managerial perfection, which seeks transfiguration thanks to the "magic" veil of empathy.

In fact, leadership manuals often emphasize that managers must communicate empathically, but simultaneously employ purely rational behavior, oriented to the task and the result.

The ethical leadership model suggests that sharing your vulnerability truly allows full harmony with others (source: Leadership: credibility and trust in leading companies, OGF Advertising).

## Non-profit Partnerships

The collaborations I am most proud of are with non-profit associations. I understand that donations and doing good are a very personal issue. Partly to step away from my professional field (I work in the world of communication), I am happy to collaborate with the associations with which I and our company collaborate.

We are currently partnered with the association APS Il Sorriso di Roma, which is "specialized" in making children and the elderly in need smile, and with SOS Villaggio dei Bambini for the long-distance adoption of less fortunate children.

As the president of APS Il Sorriso rightly says, "Do good, and good will come back to you." This couldn't be more true.

# Conclusion

With this story of my life, I hope to have given people useful ideas for pursuing financial freedom, and to have given the less fortunate tools for better fighting a horrible disease such as cancer.

This is especially true for the younger ones who often have the strength and opportunity to pursue their own path.

As I said, work is a fundamental part of a person's life, both in terms of time and commitment. Finding something you like can make a real difference in how you live.

For example, I appreciate Monday to Friday more than the weekend, as they are more dynamic. Of course, I don't mind relaxing a bit, dedicating my time to sports and my passions on Saturdays and Sundays, but I also enjoy the work week.

It's important to always keep in mind that life is unpredictable, even if you sometimes feel great, almost invincible. We all hope to be healthy and live as long as possible; however, as can be seen from my story, you can be the victim of a serious illness at any time.

This led me to think, "Live your life as if it were the last day": don't always put your goals and actions off until tomorrow, because life is unique.

What's more, one of the hardest moments for me as well as for many others has been the Covid 19 pandemic in the world, and the subsequent decrees to combat it.

I do not agree with all the measures taken, in my opinion there is a risk of making the economy, the future of our children, our healthcare and social relations suffer more than necessary. However, I would like to clarify that I am not a denier; I simply think that not everyone should be affected, only those who don't respect the rules.

I generally don't take the middle ground: people either love me or hate me, fortunately more the former than the latter. With this autobiography, I also hope to bring a bit of optimism into a difficult situation like that of the pandemic.

Many companies have gone bankrupt and many people are in difficulty due to the waves of Covid 19. In general, the digital field has not suffered; indeed, it is likely that some of people's habits and customs have changed and their "mistrust" towards digitization has been somewhat reduced.

Getting your hands dirty, having a more positive attitude, always staying up to date with studies and skills, leaving schools open, I think these are all good ways to restore our strength and help the planet in general.

For those who would like to contact me and further discuss business topics or for those looking for some health advice, I can be found on Linkedin:

https://www.linkedin.com/in/dariorabozzi/

# Acknowledgements

I want to thank my mother for this book, who gave me the idea to to write it, and my daughter Amelia, who has always been my muse.